ABCs
OF BABY ANIMALS

St. Clair Shores, Michigan

By Elizabeth Gauthier

1st Edition
Text & Design © 2020 Elizabeth Gauthier
Images used with permission from Adobe Stock

For information about permissions
please write Gauthier Publications at:

Gauthier Publications
P.O. Box 806241
Saint Clair Shores, MI 48080
Attention: Permissions Department

Frog Legs Ink is an imprint of Gauthier Publications
www.FrogLegsInk.com

Proudly printed and bound in the USA

ISBN: 978-1-942314-75-2

Library of Congress information on file

Aa

Armadillo
I have an armored shell built in!

Bb

Bunnies

Some bunnies stay small but some get as big as a small puppy!

Cc

We are cats but when we are babies we are called kittens!

Cats

Dd

Deer

Some deer have antlers!

Ee

Echidna

I am born from an egg and grow up in a pouch!

Ff

Fox
I am called a pup while I'm a baby!

Gg

Giraffe

My tongue is
blue!

Hh

Hedgehog

I curl in a ball when I'm scared.
My pokey spines protect me!

Ii

Indian
Elephant

I weigh around
200 pounds as a baby!

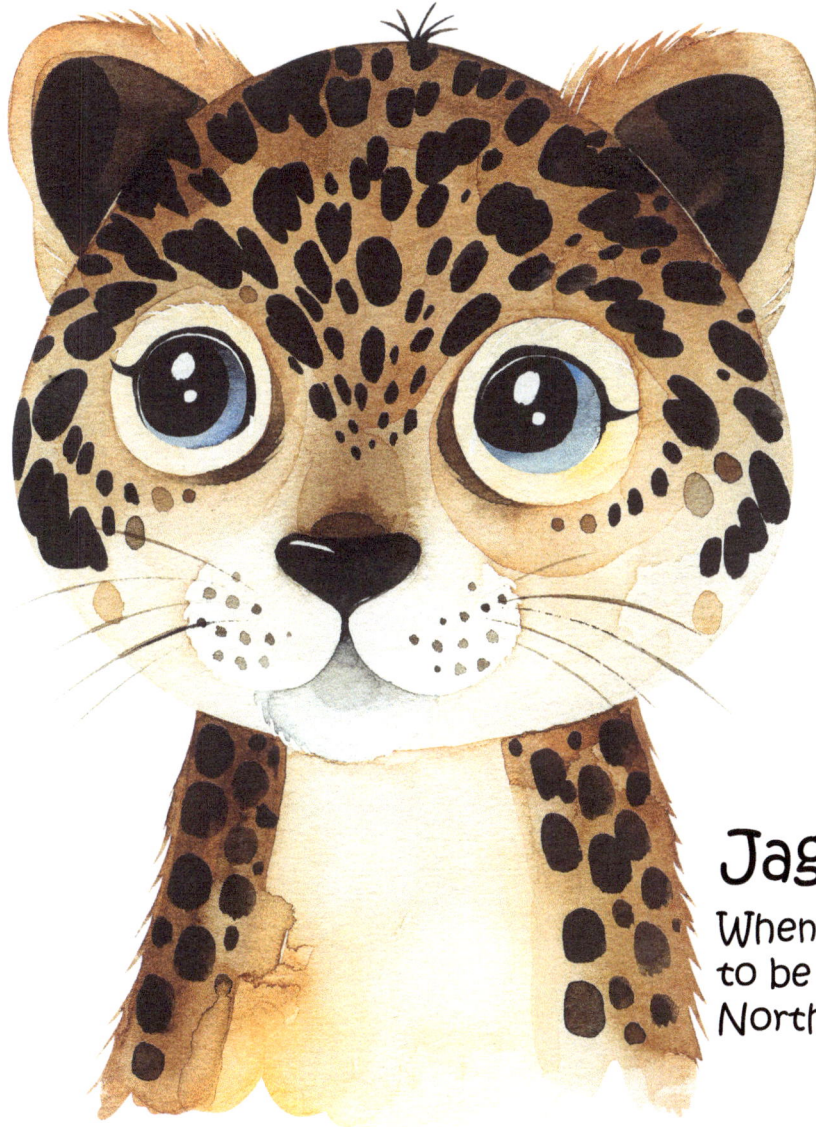

Jj

Jaguar

When I grow up I'm going to be the biggest cat in North America!

Kk

Koala

I am not a bear, I'm a marsupial!

Ll

Lioness

I'm called a cub as a baby!

Mm

Meerkat

I live in the
Kalahari Desert!

Nn

Numbat

I eat termites!

Oo

Owl

I love nighttime!

Pp

Pig
I roll in mud so
I don't get a sunburn!

Qq

Quail

I live in an egg until
I'm ready to hatch!

Rr

Raccoon

I am very smart!

Ss

Skunk

When I get scared
I let off a stinky
smell to protect me!

Tt

Three-toed sloth

I live in trees!

Uu

Urial

I have two big horns!

Vv

Vampire Bat

I sleep upside down!

Ww

Wallaby

I eat plants and can go a really long time without water!

Xx

Xerus

I'm a type of squirrel!

Yy

Yak

I like really cold weather!

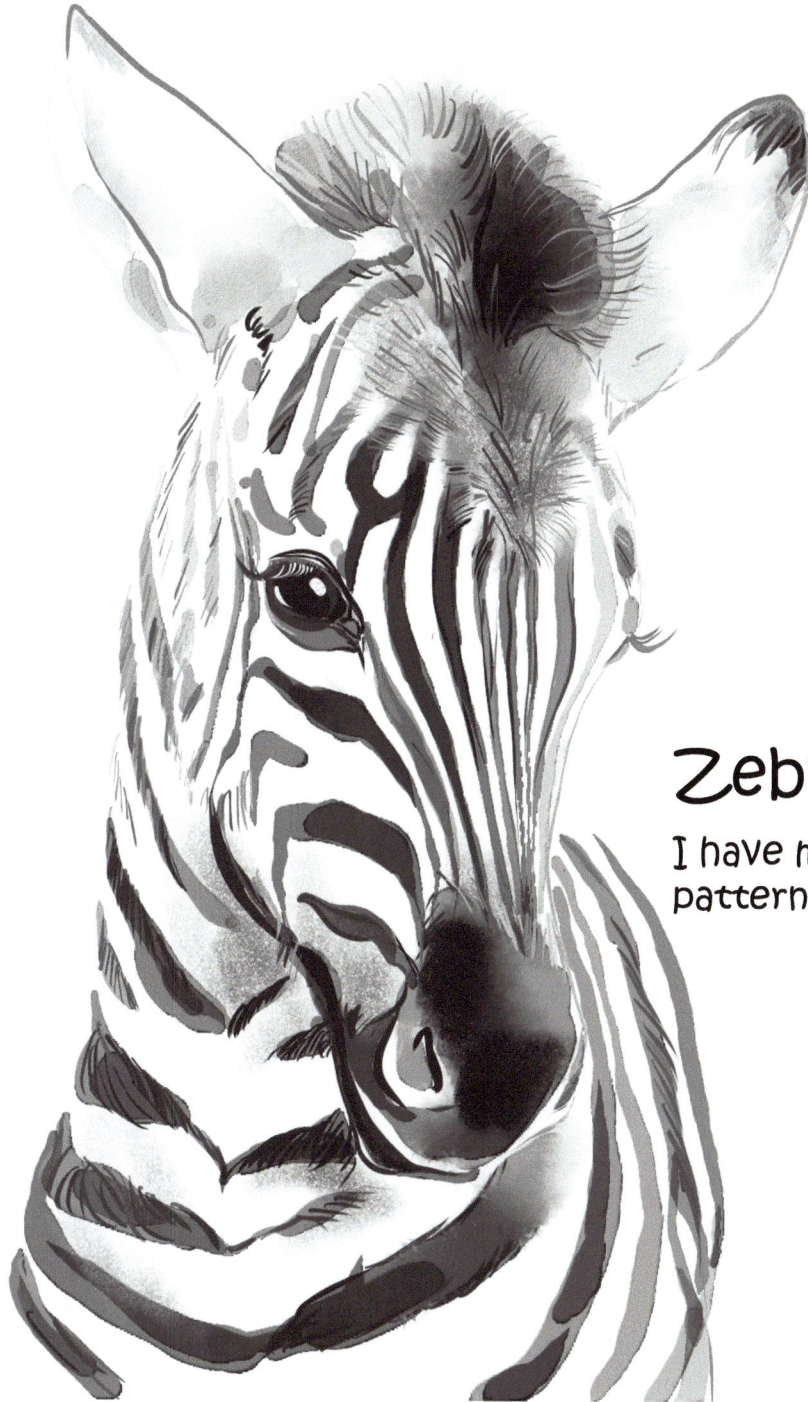

Zz

Zebra

I have my own special pattern of stripes!

ABCs OF HALLOWEEN

ABCs OF THE SEA

ABCs OF BUGS

By Elizabeth Gauthier

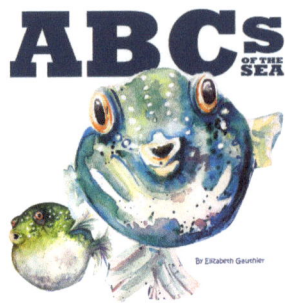

Look for additional activities & lesson plans!

1 2 3 with me series
by Elizabeth Gauthier

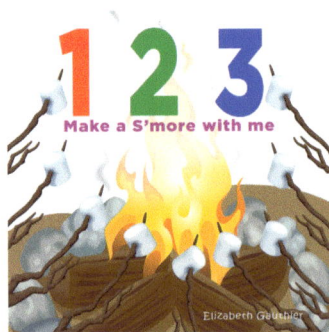

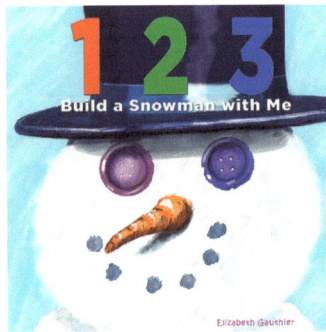

1 2 3 Make a S'more with me
Elizabeth Gauthier

1 2 3 Build a Snowman with Me
Elizabeth Gauthier

1 2 3 Visit the circus with me
Elizabeth Gauthier

1 2 3 Go to School with me
Elizabeth Gauthier

1 2 3 Carve a pumpkin with me
Elizabeth Gauthier

1 2 3 Make a Banana Split with me
By Elizabeth Gauthier

www.ingramcontent.com/pod-product-compliance
Lightning Source LLC
Chambersburg PA
CBHW042117040426
42449CB00002B/74